The Man Grave

Also by Christopher Salerno

Sun & Urn
ATM
Minimum Heroic
Whirligig

The Man Grave

Poems

Christopher Salerno

A Karen & Michael Braziller Book

Persea Books / New York

Persea Books, Inc.
90 Broad Street
New York, New York 10004

Library of Congress Cataloging-in-Publication Data
Names: Salerno, Christopher, 1975– author.
Title: The man grave : poems / Christopher Salerno.
Description: New York : A Karen & Michael Braziller Book / Persea Books, [2021] |
    Summary: "Winner of the 2020 Lexi Rudnitsky Editor's Choice Award"—Provided
    by publisher.
Identifiers: LCCN 2021016845 | ISBN 9780892555376 (paperback)
Subjects: LCGFT: Poetry.
Classification: LCC PS3619.A435 M36 2021 | DDC 811/.—dc23
LC record available at https://lccn.loc.gov/2021016845

First edition
Printed in the United States of America
Designed by Rita Lascaro

Acknowledgments

Many thanks to the following magazines in which some of these poems have appeared:

American Poetry Review	"In Memoriam"
	"Some History of Field Work"
Bennington Review	"You'll Never Get To Sleep Now"
	"Deathbed Sext"
Colorado Review	"Blue Yodel #9"
	"Don't You Have a Favorite Hour?"
Iowa Review	"We're Laughing But We've Seen a Darkness"
Jubilat	"Post Op"
Los Angeles Review	"Horror Script"
New York Times Magazine	"In Vitro" / "IVF"
New Republic	"The Reenactment"
New England Review	"Rotation"
North American Review	"Horoscope for Gemini Men"
Plume	"Best Fever Ever," "Shoulder Season,"
	"Ten Ways To Kno. . . . ," "Birds Before Bees"
Quarterly West	"Notes for Further Study"
Rhino	"Headfirst"
Verse Daily	"The Byronic Method"
Willow Springs	"Men Who Won't Travel"

Deep thanks to Gabriel Fried and the entire Persea Books team for believing in this book and for doing such a fine job shepherding it into existence. Thank you to Kelsea Habecker, whose love, grace, brilliance, and emotional labor helped make the writing of these poems possible. Thank you to William Paterson University, with special thanks to my English Department colleagues who are truly the best of the best.

Immense gratitude to the incomparable Maggie Smith for selecting *Deathbed Sext* (a chapbook containing several poems that form the core of *The Man Grave*) as the winner of the 2020 Two Sylvias Press Chapbook award. Special thanks to Kelli Russell Agodon and Annette Spaulding-Convy for publishing the chapbook at Two Sylvia Press.

Contents

III. The Heart is Wet, You are Only Sick

The Man Grave

"I used to have a cat, an old fighting tom, who would jump through the open window by my bed in the middle of the night and land on my chest. I'd half-awaken. He'd stick his skull under my nose and purr, stinking of urine and blood. Some nights he kneaded my bare chest with his front paws, powerfully, arching his back, as if sharpening his claws, or pummeling a mother for milk. And some mornings I'd wake in daylight to find my body covered with paw prints in blood; I looked as though I'd been painted with roses."

—Annie Dillard, *Pilgrim at Tinker Creek*

"What cannot be said will be wept."

—Sappho

I.
We Always Were
The Dying Type

HEADFIRST

Just a boy then, I was struck
      hard by a car and arced over

the roadside. Despite the pain I told
      no one. How the man driving

kept on driving. I hadn't yet found out
      about the body or velocity

or what a wound is, and how some bruises
      flower, spread like steam on the mirror

blurring all beauty. My mother
      says the '80s were terribly rapey.

She hisses into her rotary phone.
      Says a man may leave his voice

inside of a stranger forever, place something
      hard as a blood-flecked stone.

When I woke in the road, I rested
      my little chrome bicycle by the curb.

The smell of lilac, the sound of traffic
      starting up again in the street.

Shapes that keep us awake decades
      later. The fuck do I know about

all this thickness? Not the slant rhyme
      of fear & underwear. Haven't I

walked around with a killer's power,
        swaggering until now? But any boy's

teen years: days spent pursuant to puberty.
        The body as factory. I would

have driven high across this enormous
        darkness just to watch a woman

unbutton air. I should be writing this
        with fear, knowing I was danger.

SOME HISTORY OF FIELD WORK

Then November seemed like a whole other gender:
the veins of wet leaves splayed upon the bedrock.
Skin of the land beneath which you could hear
your own blood rushing boyhood out. Under orders now
to *be a man,* I lie down on a large nurse tree, a fallen log
feeding the rest of the forest with its body; long scar
down birch bark. *Please let this be enough.* After awhile
I get hungry, too, my tongue a useless fruit. But I will lie
here until something sings *be this.* Birds, back me up—
you who leave your first feathers in the brambles.
For years, men had to hide their porn in the woods.
Desire in exile, insects running in rows. We boys
quickly gathering in the reedy ditch to see. Little hands—
we were hardly what the ladybugs were looking for.
But we held the centerfold sideways until it was taken
by the wind. Only by waiting did we come to wanting.
Now, there are switches in the air; I can't stay here.
The trout grow so cold they leap into the trees, become
the stars above this boreal forest. Still, I
would like to *be a man,* to see what that might lead to.

SPORTS NO ONE FOLLOWS

Standing in the septic field I fire
      the .45 into the woodpile that runs

along the tree line like a train
      then come bumblebees big

as eyeballs and my grandfather whacks
      six with a badminton racket

down they go into the wet crabgrass
      me too young to reload the gun

I don't know who invented violence
      but how's this for manly: a long

drawn-out war during which some of us
      will die with our eyes open.

THE REENACTMENT

What mattered in early wars
was the cavalry marching through
deep muck, the fife & drums,
stern ravens, words called out
across small, stagnant ponds.
They tell us every landscape longs
to be a battlefield. Someone
fires a cannon the size of a cave,
and we watch as shockwaves
italicize the trees. We, the living,
try channeling the original grief.
But this battle is nothing like
I thought it would be. I have little
idea what it takes to hold a field,
why someone might like to dress up
as the dead, those blown forward
in a crowd of men. Quick fuse:
young man with a bandage
and a period gun sings an anthem
from the archive, steps through
a cloud of cannon smoke.
White sight. A horse-drawn
darkroom rumbles by. A butterfly
flags. The gods never arrive.

BETA MALE NOTEBOOK

A stepladder to the sublime. That's how I try to leave manliness behind.

Outside, I sprinkle lime around the blue hydrangea
so that next year's flowers will come back pink.

I take the thin path through the woods to smell the reservoir, to hear
  woodpeckers
drum the trunks of poplars.

I mistake the change in light for a change in myself.
This is one day. I'm stumbling down through generations of men.

I sit on a log and google my uncle's mug shot. I google my cousin's mug
  shot.
From this log I google three of my great uncles' mug shots.
Cigar guys with big cars and eyes ablaze.

This is almost a poem. It goes something like this: I love soft moss under
  my feet.
My steps leave a trail of ellipses across the yard where I walk out to
  surrender
this manliness to the moon, but the moon is already gone.

There is no breaking out of nature. I used to think the moon-landing
  meant
the moon would land on us, that it meant us harm.

I come from dummies. Tonight I float a doughnut in a bowl of full-fat
  milk.
I google how to be more tender, then I read about the marbling
on premium cuts of beef.

I sniff both my armpits. I burp the word *nerds*. It's a quarter to five. Is it
   too late to go shopping for a father?

I get further into folklore. In the end my own father refused to give his
   pain a number, would simply stare at the doctor.

Question: brother, was that you weeping in your shed this morning
or were you overcome by varnish fumes?

How old is your beard? Did you get a deer this year?
Would I need a .35 to take down a moose?

Has the past been talking to you? Show me where you're buried.

MEN WHO WON'T TRAVEL

Snowplows
smack the manhole
all morning long.
Inconsolable crows
rise and reset. What
I have memorized
is moving again:
winter sun hitting
the substation fence—
a rubric for evening
as December strains after
its own vanishment.
Once the pigeons return
to the rooftops at dusk
having proven their part
in the natural history
of distance, I will eat
a pink grapefruit
from a faraway place,
pinch the little wooden
seed and whisper to it
the word, *Tallahassee,*
which is the name of
the city where they
discovered the sun.
I would like to go there
but I am impossible
to move, like a canoe
packed with snow,
a thing you only row
with your eyes.

ONE OF THESE DAYS, ALICE

My Uber driver's knuckle
tattoos read *BANG*
     and *ZOOM*. We only get
          so many syllables. A nervous

student emails to ask, *Can I
use I* in this essay about the wild
     parakeets of Brooklyn?
          Parakeets who broke loose

from their cages long ago
and have claimed this place
     as a home ever since.
          The driver's young daughter,

riding up front, says, *Daddy, I
want to go home.* She pokes his
     forearm bruise. He says, *Sweetie, no.*
          Daddy needs you to man up now.

And I watch as her spirit is
sucked into a passing cloud
     drifting toward the moon.
          The average cloud weighs

a million or so pounds,
yet planes fly right through.
     Our car climbs the steep
          hill out of the cavity of the city,

city this child will someday
flee. Do not tell us
      her leaving isn't a form
            of faith. Some would give

a wing to be unbound, to move
      through new leaves, sing
            that old song of being new.

SPORTS NO ONE FOLLOWS

Sky the color of which Gatorade flavor?
We guess at the metabolism of clouds
by measuring our shadows on the wet playground.
So this is the lithosphere. We can hear them
sliding, the tectonic plates, genderless
as panes of polished glass in the underground
museum of men's loneliness for men,
which houses only the sound of air rushing out
of a deflating ball, like the hiss of a goose
when you've gotten too close,
who won't let you pass until you make your soft
little sound of subordination. Don't
be afraid. No one else will witness this, the lull
of your life. Here, all evening, trees will reach
toward and away from each other
because of wind. They, too, do their best
to never let themselves be touched
or admit that their bodies have teamed
up in dreams. Don't tell me
you love only the wide silence that's been
imprinted in our code when you've seen
the catalogue trapped in winter branches,
the soccer goal gaping with shame.

CRAWLING BACK

Thick sycamores hold up the sky
as I fastwalk across the avenue, and before
I know what's real a pickup drives by
and a man with his face in the window-slit
as if someone expelling smoke yells out
FAGGOT. The hub caps of his crew-cab truck
spin the daylight round. The jogger
ten sidewalk squares ahead maintains his stride
and I wonder which one of us is the *faggot.*
There are a million soldier ants spilling out
of the sidewalk crack to walk the unbroken chain
of pheromones. I watch my step. Don't we
grow cruel if we are not careful? I spot the feral
tuxedo cat who once a week visits our yard
to taunt my indoor tom at the glass back door.
I watch a giant frown of a cloud dissolve
over downtown. How easy to let that
red word fall in the road behind me like
the boorish little boy I used to be when
my body was just one of many theories floating
over the fifth-grade schoolyard where
we all so commonly called each other *fag*
that if you said it loud every boy standing
on the playground would turn his head around.

HORROR SCRIPT

At school we studied the mysteries
of the amygdala. The self

       and its contingencies. If you've ever
       cupped a lizard in your hands

you understand interiors.
Or a housefly, that little sinner no one loves—

       its greatest fear is not enough air.
       This one dying in the windowsill

buzzes back to life at dusk
when whoever keeps calling

       just breathes and hangs up. All evening
       a black Saab idles in your street.

Somewhere in the night you bleed
on the sheets, wake again,

       your fear a thing to rise into.

SPORTS NO ONE FOLLOWS

To learn how to shut another man's mouth
you must point at him with the fat end of the bat,
tell him he is beautiful inside and out. Or go
talk to my cousin, in prison for assault.
You don't have to forgive his cumbrous hands
for what they have done: sever someone's optic nerve.
Tonight, I'll watch the ballgame until I see
the shortstop punch a fist into his mitt
in the top of the ninth, after his fielding error
sends the hometown crowd for the door.
Coach stepping from the cinderblock cage
points to the infield players, pulls both
of his earlobes then slides a hand down each
forearm clean. This is a private matter
between them. A poem for the season of
flowering and shame. This is early yet, still spring
training, before the tulips all fall apart,
before the daffodils shut their stupid little mouths.

IN THE DRUNKHOUSE MUSEUM

Always someone's uncle blowing across
        the mouth of a bottle. Tuning a black dial

for a temporary song. The saints
        marching in and out, waking the sky

by dying young. *My life, my liver.*
        This brine that taught us how to lie,

turned my tongue into an arrow
        in my mouth. Do you like the taste

of afterlife? Tell me everything you know
        about staying alive without liquor.

When the bottle-green night empties
        into drains, all across the city

our people appear. Outside the stadium
        after the game, my stepfather insisting

time to make our way home.
        He drives like shit beneath the unblinking

moon still lost in the east, one blood
        shot eye refusing to shut. Some days

I'd lean in and measure his breath.
        Did it burn your hair like dry barley hay?

Had he started back quoting
        the wind to the wind? I never did learn

to swallow the unsayable things,
        so he worked those words out of me.

To be drowned out or knocked against.
        What I do is cock a shotgun

in my head, say no more, pour it all out.
        Last week, my uncle snuck away to buy

a pint at midnight, was struck
        in the crosswalk on his walk back.

The front teeth of a jeep, taking the hill
        too fast, hit the nightcap first, then poured

out the contents of his wonderful skull.

II.
Deathbed Sext

IN MEMORIAM

An only boy may have
    had to play with god.
        Both of them beings
            as quiet as glue. I put

my nose to the sound
    hole in a mahogany guitar,
        inhale the wood which
            never really dies. Like violets

pressed in a hymnal
    never die. Count me
        among those mourners
            singing all the wrong songs.

DEATHBED SEXT

We always were the dying type.
Diagnosed early with *bon voyage*. As a boy
    I heard a murder
    ballad on the radio. Talk about
breaking the body into song!
    Like a budding sicko
I sang along. Beneath every boy's brainstem
    is a provisional gland. A full array
of rare emo registers.
    Why a man in a barber's chair
    will stare deeply into his own eyes.
Comically big comb in the far corner of the room.
    It's just a life. One adjusts
    one's genitals in the empty elevator.
One adjusts
    a cluster of stars. When parts of us
need lifting up, I don't blame
    biology. But I wonder about
        our need for the irrational ritual.
    I watch M tape a clean
    maxi pad over the peep-
hole in her hotel door—
    is this about anonymity, not
    being seen? In our bodilessness
do *we* ever truly disappear?
    You can pay to receive
five texts a day that say, *Don't forget*
    you are going to die.
Device returned to its factory settings.
        The complete black of before.

What disquiets me now
            is not corporeal.
        It's the boredom on the faces
of the people on the streets
            of New York City.
        Send me pics of you eating a feeling.
        The three-layer cake of it.
I'm sending you the city at noon:
        day
                drunk
                        brunch
                bros
        lower
                east
                        side.
Young guy slips his elbow in jelly.
        Another puts a finger in his beer foam.
            Sidewalk dog startled
            by sudden saxophone. White
wrapper rising in
the puerile wind. Here's the condom I found
        on the floor of a midtown taxi.
One more dollop of lewdness
        for the fearhole. As kids we used
to talk about the fuck that flies,
        about the Hail Mary lay.
I want to waltz with you away from what
        once was monstrously male
        about me but I also
            want to survive.

You send me the forehead
with a palm on it.

From the Met I send a photograph
of an ancient Greek statue,
the amazing arc of its ass
lit by late-afternoon light.
Not even the gods look away.

DICKINSONIAN PICS

I heard a phone buzz when I died.
Your sext lit up the larger darkness.
Bright as a swan or a wild syllable
lost to lust. How many men slip

into abandon, grow sick with kink. I had
taken my temperature, gotten one last look
at the zoomed-in moon, then felt
a vibration. I rushed to see the screen:

there interposed a photo of a lady
bug perched on the thong
of your sandal where it rested
from the stresses of the air. Maybe

there is too little structure
in seduction, like a loose scarf
taking to the sky. All day I look
out windows clouded by breath,
misjudge the nearness of lust & death.

ADVICE CONTAINING MOSTLY IMPRESSIVE BELCHES

Don't be the boy who eats things for money.
Don't listen at doors or you'll be seized
by the hair. Don't let the pitch of your voice
lift too high around other guys. As you reach
into your lover's coveralls beside the dead
poet's tomb, remember to mention the monarch
butterflies, the tulips torn apart by fastidious
rain. If the conversation lags, don't say *A penis
for your thoughts*. It would be lovelier to say
The wine is on the table breathing. Personify desire
only when love threatens to do less. You must
carry a square of cloth to dab at the blood
should your zipper catch on the vestigial
genitals, place where your lover's words
once were. Didn't they ever teach you how
a word works? How its wings can operate
in any old wedge of sky as long as you be
a voyaging body. You will find your new language
in the *V* of a tree, carve your initials into
its thick trunk, male metaphor of slow growing.
To see a man without his hair is nothing—
to see a tree without its bark is sycamore.
You must try not to speak when your face
is in lather. Try not to sob at parades.
When you say your final words of the day
to your god, ask her to lay her august thing down
along the man line. Tonight, as the raccoons
gather on the neighbor's roof at dusk,
light yourself some lamps. Before
it gets so dark you can't even see your sewing.

FEAR OF MAKING OUT

He taps a spider
web with a fork, tears
a hole in a cocoon
with a stone. He goes
out for a pass
on the lawn to meet
the evening moths
head on. Past the bed
sheets billowing
on the line, he stands
at the far edge of
an almost sexless dream,
a June storm
rolling in, a certain
irritation on his skin,
the lightning bug he
allows to crawl his leg.
When will the bio-
luminescence in these
fireflies be used
to make a medicine? Pills
that subtract one
of the five senses or
a pill that dims
the loins of teens?
Once, there were limits
to joy. Later, more
loveliness came.
He ate a pink icing
rose from the corner
of the cake, yet all
he tasted was face

when he finally made out
and with a girl
he'd never even met
in a gravel lot and leaning
against a fruit-born tree,
its white blossoms blaring
as blaring trumpets do
to warn these lovers
you will be devoured too
as sure as sunset dissolves
down the throat of dusk
like the day's medication,
the evening-after pill.

NOTES FOR FURTHER STUDY

You are a nobody
until another man leaves
a note under your wiper:
I like your hair, clothes, car—call me!
Late May, I brush pink
crepe myrtle blossoms
from the hood of my car.
Again spring factors
into our fever. Would this
affair leave any room for error?
What if I only want
him to hum me a lullaby?
To rest in the nets
of our own preferences?
I think of women
I've loved who, near the end,
made love to me solely
for the endorphins. Praise
be to those bodies lit
from gland to gland. I pulse
my wipers, sweep away pollen
from the windshield glass
to allow the radar
detector to detect. In the prim
light of spring I drive
home alone along the river's
tight curves where it bends
like handwritten words.
On the radio, a foreign love
song some men sing to rise.

THE DOUBLE IMAGE

I had sexted Anne Sexton and was stricken
with remorse & shamefacedness. No, this dream

> was not about the flesh-and-blood Anne
> Sexton, but about man's inner woman, the *Anima*.

They said I'd never get her back, not with my eyes
in keyholes or by waiting for something small

> to dilate. Everyone wants to know
> what I felt after she left me palimpsestic—

her outline still visible against the wall
like some painted-over apostle. But I only fell

> into endless confession like what the trees are doing
> right now budding out their forelocks

for spring. I stand to watch the forsythia in its flare,
and the season having its portrait done

> with such superlatives reminds me again
> how lost I am when Anne does not appear.

THE BYRONIC METHOD

There is no code or corrective shoe.
Only raspberries to cover the tips of my thumbs.

       When I sexted you a snorkel you sexted me a squid.
       Finally, a language for our modified love.

That spring I sexted the hell out of spires, ants on bananas,
some honeysuckle I saw in Syracuse. What else

       counterfeits like lust? A fire escape, a fluid sky.
       The endless ache of our minor works. I wanted to see

a distance, but through *your* eyes. When I sexted you
a telescope you sexted me the moon.

TEN WAYS TO KNOW HOW HE FEELS ABOUT YOU

When a man loves an omen
nothing can be done. You wait
all day to hear your name,
for the sentence and its syntax
to lie down together.

***

Your man puts a noun
where there is none. Animal
mineral vegetable sex. He takes
you to the river, makes a flat pebble
skip across the water.

***

Says he's living in an allegory, asks
that you wait for it to play out,
for his luck to take hold. He hands
you an afghan and a dented
canteen full of chilled gin.

***

While he's off buying stamps
you study his wallpaper:
faraway windmills rotating shyly
in a countryside. You rise,
try leaving, but the Victorian doorknob
comes away in your hand.

***

Everything is a piece

of something else. The clothes
you remove like chaff, trying to hang up
your hang ups. A body is for
forming or for going,
he says, on a spree.

***

Takes a girl by surprise. Using your wrist
as a hinge he spins you
on your heels, his leather cuff smudging
your smokey eye. You both
pitch south.

***

But the era of omens isn't over.
All day he speaks of oxblood, runes,
Homeric doves flying
to the right. You say *only in music
are there such heavy rests.*
He hands you the hands of a clock
which you press into a book.

***

Here is your lover in a larger pattern:
late-afternoon shadows on a sheet. The space
between clouds. The fluid
sky fat with joy
and also blue beyond reason.

***

He renames you *thee,*
asks *aren't we sparks?* At the dive
bar he sticks his finger
in your beer foam, dares you
to take him home.

***

The lover's leap, you think,
leaving your axis like you're in a ballet.
Perhaps tonight he will finally say
your name. But he comes riding a piano
into the room, begs you to listen
to his next baritone vow.

A MAN NAMING A FEELING

A man walks into an emotion, sits down and orders a word. Word-
    tender brings him
a bowl of chestnuts, a glossary, a glass of amaro.

The man's been married to blackouts. Like the dark-eyed birds that
    smack the windows
of his house while trying to fly through.

There are rituals he did not know he knew. He walks his blind Retriever
    through the
graveyard at dusk. Stone after stone. Confused by the beauty of a
    memory

blurred by grief, until, finally, overhead, the sound of honking geese.

Some punchlines take us a year to hear. A man walks into a bar
with a pocketful of rusty nails. He will bury the nails beneath his wife's
    pink hydrangea.
The acid in the rust will force next year's flowers

to come back blue. Some days it's a little darker than this.

A man walks into an emotion, sits down and orders a word. His beard
    has grown
all the way to his belt. These chestnuts, he says, are as smooth as the butt
    of my grandfather's rifle.

But what do you feel, the word-tender asks.
Like geese on a darn sheet of ice. Like all my dogs are running in
    diagonals.

Ah, so you feel grief or hurt or horror, the word-tender says.

Lost, the man looks at himself in a spoon. His ears are two parentheses inside of which sit the bleached bones of nouns.

IVF

More snow fell than was able
to be plowed. We turned
our faces to the clouds, waited
in waiting rooms to fill
out the forms, kissing each
one like the scalp of a child
with hair as unreal
as a doll built by hand
in the hold of a beautiful ship.
I sit in the room full of porn,
exhale my own name,
the one of that saint who
carried the Christ child
over a swollen river.

MISTER UNIVERSE

Even you remember ruin. Time your sister carved
a flute from one of your bones. Mother drew
a zigzag mustache under your nose, made you learn
violin. And you raised your elbow to make the bow
sound, then slid the violin beneath the stucco house.
It took only a few words out of a girl's mouth
to split your hips in two, your skinny boy body
made funny: arms and legs like narrow streets.
Now, for love you would not give a rib
or sing your sin. But these muscles you build
from pills will do. Soon, your shoulders widen
like a big ship's wake. When you open your mouth
a fat muscle flops out. You are bent on bending
the tendons to your will, on being built.
Which of our muscles comes alive when we quake?
Psoas? Iliopsoas? Crossing the pelvic floor
like two ropes in dark silt where sorrow
sorrow sorrow sits deeper than any marrow.

IVF

Under a sky drunk with gray, I arrive
to the office park's row of black windows.
Overhead, a swoop of Swallows
maneuvers at height, and I want that
flight to be my own flight. But I am here
pressing a vial of sterile sample
against my ribs, hoping to keep it viable
for the hour. When the doctor says *look,*
I step into the beige corridor, peer
into the microscope where zillions of
my anonymized sperm freak, ride
across glass. I'm here to account for
those wobbly or frail sperm that veer
like the shopping cart with a shitty wheel,
steering away from a world already
too full as we head into winter:
foghorns, pine barrens, very brave birds.
Within an hour this batch will be
given a grade for morphology, motility,
then a rough total count. Of those
that would dance until they wear
themselves out, only one will be
injected into the egg, the egg put back
fat to try. One more story of the body.
My eye against the microscope lens
is the beginning or the end.

AN OLD MAN CURSING A FOX

I can't tell you how vivid
the sorrow of a whole life
seems moments after seeing
a fox gnaw a young groundhog
stomach full of sour cherries.
Better if the Bobwhites do
not call faintly to each other
in the underbrush. Better to be wary
of the trotting fox, who guide
books say will never relax. Today
you see him dragging a pair
of antlers over your far meadow.
In the sun one antler is glistening
with sap. You hold at the tree
line, watch this illicit fox-task
unfold. You try shouting at him
to stop. You whip your wet scarf
against an oak and still the fox
does not look up. You shout
at him with all you've got, your
terrible dream from last night
about what this world cannot afford.

POST OP

A man I know receives ten bees
by mail each week.
His wife takes one by one
by the wings, lets them sting him
along the spine to raise
his body's immune response.
How like a weed he must seem
to those bees, giving only a drop
of his sour blood back.
For months my mother had to turn
a tiny key to widen
the plastic palate glued
to the roof of my middle school mouth,
the year I told her I was ready
to raise myself. But when I woke
in the hospital after one more operation,
my stitches fiendishly itchy,
I wondered what history costs the body,
and if all our previous minutes
are still in us, why not roll
up the skin, squeeze
out all the air to make room
for more? Once the gauze
was taken off, layer upon oniony layer
removed, I was carried outside
where the ornamental cherry trees
of the Upper East Side
bloomed, and city bees seeking
certain immediacies burrowed
into the mouths of those flowers
trembling now from the weight

of all that frantic work,
and I begged each bee to sting
its strongly worded missive
into me in my post-op opioid haze.

WE'RE LAUGHING BUT WE'VE JUST SEEN A DARKNESS

After growing up I grew an ear
for that note of sadness hidden in laughter.

        We assume all sorrow is redacted there.
        We trust the mouth as a medium

but often the louvers of anguish
don't make a good seal, causing the laughter

        we hear to carry a second sound
        overheard, as with the whistling of radiator

steam, hearing heat inside
the pipe like some darkness in the larynx.

        It's not a musical note and not
        not an echo either. When two people fall

into insuppressible laughter, brut
champagne pouring out of their noses,

        one may not be able to stop, may
        even need help getting up off the floor.

IVF

Then we froze the embryos like god
forsaken things. We wished upon

pharmaceutical stars. Never ask what fails
what it wants to be. Always *a vacancy.*

They filled our empty holes with needles
at autumn's end. They took our blood

which overflowed, formed a cold river
splitting two cities. It's hardly morbid

when nothing is even born. Later,
we'll go blind below the waist. Bodies

two nests swept from the eaves.
Yes, loss is full of new laws: I wake

each morning and in the space
between my legs a fruit bat hangs.

DAILY BREAD

The dough is proving
someplace warm.
At dawn I stretch my
morning stretch,
transform my spine
into a xylophone.
I sext you the center
of a cinnamon bun.
You sext me a fork
on the floor. I sext
you a stuntman standing
inside a cannon,
and you sext me a really
long fuse. I think
I am ready to cry
in other colors.
Let us boil our rings
in river water.
Let us sit at this
table and eat.

III.
The Heart Is Wet,
You Are Only Sick

AT THE FARM STAND DURING THE SOLAR ECLIPSE

Aren't hens dear? How they squat
if willing to be picked up. Other-
wise, may run. *You know how it is,*

says my most masculine friend.
To know a thing, we want to
touch it. I reach down to try a hen.

It scoots, wings raised like blades,
the sign for *no.* We've all seen them
sort of fly away: those mock-flights

that don't hold air. Embodying
perhaps our own flight patterns:
low over black water where the axe

sits lodged in the stump. I should be
less afraid of love. I hear
the laughter of women drifting

from the barn, see the changing sky
full-sized over the coop—a farm's
greatest truth. What I want to know:

how to fall out of love without
feeling like a fool. That's the dark
side of desire, I know, but we have

arrived here in time to witness
a rare solar eclipse. In the fields around,
acres of corn slap shut their husks.

Not even noon but the entire farm
is going dark, and every last hen,
from instinct, returning to the coop.

PORTRAIT MODE

That post-electro-shock therapy look
on my grandmother's face. Her mornings
in the yellow world we called them.
Cheekbones a pair of minimalist stills
lit by an antediluvian light
like the two pale orchids I bring to the edge
of death and back each month.
What has happened could happen again.
Decades of dependence on medicine
and men. Husband in his siren-blue
uniform and badge. Wife whatever pink
pill is in her palm, and dreaming
of the driveway. One day she climbs
into the oak tree's dark spokes
with her string of real pearls, rips the strand
letting each pearl fall like hail
against the hood of his parked patrol car.
We call this survival, confusing oneself
for a cloud spilling its affliction.
And the moment he draws his revolver
on his own kids in the kitchen
you can just make out the sound of
my grandmother's gasp, about as loud
as some flowers being torn in half.

ROTATION

The cornstalks seem happy just standing there all summer.
Until someone calls time money, rain adjusts the river,
and shall we rotate the crops? My family
spoke Polish, came from farms. I've seen
the black-and-whites of haystacks and tried to guess
if it was end of summer, and why are the farmer's wives
wearing their pinafore aprons in the field?
Sometimes, in an off-year, a single stalk of corn
shoots up among the knee-high soybean.
They call this a *volunteer*. What wants out of the past
will come: something, someone, some-
horse, somecrow, somewren. But I am nothing
if not New World. As I bite a cold radish,
place an iron key on the back of my neck trying
to halt a nose bleed, I curse the landscape
of my face, the lineage in its shape,
the jawline like a beam or some similar part of a barn—
mother's father's features from way back
when farm was only an extension of continent,
and the light of the world keeps going.

BEST FEVER EVER

Dawn's got a choreography.
When the tall grass shakes out

the night bird and starts
a young coyote howling in a ring

of redwood trees. Nothing
can prepare you for waking up.

Not a too-loud owl. Not the mid-
night special unzipping the dark.

We can't blame our eyes
for opening. Though there are muscles

in the body we never even use.
A Nijinsky of nothingness is what

I am thinking of. Or the rabbit
not hopping under the streetlamp.

Or a moth found flat in the pages
of a paperback. You shake it

into the empty bucket beside the bed,
which only confuses the plot

of the book as it lurches you
forward and backward in time.

YOU'LL NEVER GET BACK TO SLEEP NOW

At school we studied conquistadors. Ways masculine
        history could be measured in missions.
    My stepfather stepping
            through a cloud
                of boat motor smoke.
    Me gnawing this blue
pen into a shiv. Missions undertaken
                despite all futility:
I was sent to fetch a crescent wrench that wasn't even there.
    Soon, we learn to line up the tools.
    Locate gears behind tiny doors. Another poem
begins: we are building an enormous tugboat
            to crisscross the sound
                with all of our unthinkable cargo
    until we've become that
            someone on the farther bank who
                isn't invited back.
Having journeyed to the cape of no more feels, I kill
                a large Coke on the beach.
Today I walked backwards into the open sea
        pulling a wave over me like
                a wine-dark cape. On the sand
stood a bride and groom in a storm

        or divorce dream. At what age
                did I learn to swim all alone in the Atlantic
                even with my lack?
        Why was I wanting to be so startled
        that I would only swim after dark?
                    Each of us offers themselves whole
                to the motion of waves,
                    to the riot of water-light, hoping to see what

no eyes can see. I have an average heart and a thin belief,
    so being woken by thunder in the middle of
        the night means
    I'll never get back to sleep.
        I'll go out where the morning is.
I'm trying to be more *woke* at work: acknowledgment of
    weather coming in, souls afloat
        in the chop offshore
        of this wherever the hell.
            With my steamer trunk
    and my telescope, this is what I found:
When the world was flat as a finished proof
        and men inched all night in wooden ships
            floating just off the coast of newish worlds
    there were mornings when the only things
        to wake some men
in their dark harbors were the waves.

LIFE INSIDE THE WHALE

What has two thumbs and stands
in the mammal's mouth, sleeps on a bed of salt?
I'm hardly the first to sound

such a big body out, to grow up like a word
in its throat. Nobody's here
but krill. The body of a whale is

mostly bow, and I woke in this bow in the dark.
Power out. Blue pilot light
unlit. Is it New Year's yet? I want to wag

my unloved parts at the moon.
Each night, the blowhole flares, bathes
the stars. I've had it with

my own desires. I know the true diagnosis
is loneliness. There pumps a hundred-pound heart
here which may never be beheld.

ON BEING ASKED NICELY TO SHAVE

A mustache is a message. A veritable
marquee. Says a body's had music in it.
Your father in the doorway hugging
his accordion knows. But I'm other men,
the sum of their weight. You know that
tiny pinch you say you feel the moment
you ovulate? How many unsaid
words, small as salt, will dissolve within
our armature, stomached at dawn
and held all day. Sun on the other side
of the house now, we stand here trying
to fold a fitted sheet. We hold it up
like a door between us. Already dusk
when you notice my face, its readable surface.
You speak your preference: for the blade
to come closer, make this face a clean stone.

DAYLIGHT SAVINGS

The extra hour's for eating old burdens up.
        Through a funnel or with forager's teeth.
To grieve what you haven't grieved,
        cumbersome as a meal swallowed whole.
After hunger drove us down a deep ravine
        to where chanterelles grow wild
in the shade, it took headlamps pointing north
        to see. We put mud on our faces, got beyond
being human, said *Dark on the day, no hour*
        is too late. It comes a time. The rest of the story
is boring: breathable air, red wine inside
        the tent, then neither one of us
could sleep. We wandered in bathrobes around
        the campground. Black bears watched
us comb each other's hair. The owls were
        too loud to be wise. Once we heard
the woods start falling apart, we got lower
        than ferns beneath liminal trees.

WATCHING NATURE TV IN MY FATHER'S HOUSE

Day starts its animals. We expect
the words will come to us.
Arms out, I copy the osprey's
means of drying its wings.
The osprey, boring in the tall air,
draws big for its descent,
is hungry for silver, dives the steep path
to water. Some birds remind us
only of before we began
to disambiguate the possibility of flight.
My father falling asleep in his
pale blue recliner, the sky inside
both of us now, if only
for half an hour. What is he
in his sleeping: the osprey,
deadly, plunging dark water,
or the minnow's mistake of resting?

BLUE YODEL #9

I wandered
lonely as a cow
across an old acre.
I knelt in the bother
for most of December.
Pissed a hole in the snow
the shape of a flower. Have I
made it any further than my father
in his laughter, before his slaughter?
Sometimes I travel so far from myself
the herd-call hits the amber mountain flat
and I forget how to lead my heavy body back.

THE PILIATED

woodpecker hammers at the chrome
chimney cap to woo a female into the zone.
His drumming drones three floors down
to the pipes of our house. I step outside to pick
up a stone, hurl it at the blue vernacular sky.
People are born with two innate fears:
one of falling and one of loud noise. The rest
of our fears come from family. At first
it's your father, or maybe a *step* who drank
or collected long guns. Mine used to bring me
to the projects as a prop, buy himself coke
while I yo-yoed alone in the unlit stretch
of grass out front where I tried but could not
quite learn how to make the yoyo sleep
until a girl my size taught me with a snap
of her wrist. And how that yo-yo spun
at the end of its string, hovered for a whole
minute above the wet grass where worms
were beginning to work their way up.

HOROSCOPE FOR GEMINI MEN

Ghost is now a noun you can verb. Yet the best
a ghost can do is flick a light, whisper
I hate my afterlife. Maybe the problem is the fluidity
of identity, that *I* is too strong a word.
Gemini, as you walk away from every lover
you miniaturize, your body becoming a dot
of light on the horizon like the barely-
visible Venus. What does all this leaving lead to?
It's like listening to the story of your own
afterlife: once the stars pull out and frost
hits the field. Honey crystalizing in the jar.
I know I know this much: you can have
the opposite of an orgasm. Your torso can rust
like the blade of a plow. All your hair
can go to seed at the end of a season. We all vie
for a view of something real—oleander or
your old selves—but don't both contain poison?
They say less wanting means more grace,
like running your finger along the fur lining
of an empty suitcase. Gemini, the heart
is wet, you are only sick. Brain swollen
as a nova above the rum and coke colored night
where half of these stars may be dead
but we still get to see them now and again.

BIRDS BEFORE BEES

I can see pretty

        far away
        with my glasses:

    the color of minor
        birds extemporizing
        in the rain-washed pine.
Strain
leaves every
    thing thinner, has
        its season. I pause in

    the middle of the
street for a bee

        passing
        on its way
        to a blossom,
one that is deep
    and pink.

MOONSHOT

I do have a past to break with.
Possibly in this very room full

       of heirloom geraniums that die
       unless we bring them inside, cut

each one back by half for winter.
We hope there is a future for

       delicate things. Poems of penance
       and limited logic written an hour

before the dark starts to exaggerate.
It's useful to say we have caused

       others to suffer. The moon glows whiter
       behind us in the mirror. And what's

the use of flying to the moon if we
are unable to cross the space that separates

       us from ourselves? May we become
       to bravery what saying is to the sentence.

This break in silence brought to you
by mistake in a room full of geranium

       pots hanging moonlike above. Where
       have we landed tonight? I take one

small, un-famous step toward my regrets
along the mind's white surface.

DON'T YOU HAVE A FAVORITE HOUR?

People rise out of the hour of day they love.
At noon I like how loudly the pink
      azaleas bloom beneath the cambered pine.
          The way our eyes auto-tune each

blade of grass into "the grass" as if a lawn
could be orchestral. This sounds like
      a line, but the deer skull lying in the briars
          contains a hive. Take no fruit there!

Let's pretend it's November, and all
the bees you've vowed to keep
      are hunkered around the heartmeat.
          Even the tree rings grow closer together.

You won't exactly be a child again, but maybe
a boy small for your age, not yet worn
      down by manliness or illness.
          Each day you'll watch the shadows clock

across the lawn. And at your favorite hour
of day you'll rise, step outside of
      the body of thought to fly your
          diamond kite in a soft-spoken wind.

About the Author

Christopher Salerno is a poet, the editor of Saturnalia Books, and Professor of Creative Writing at William Paterson University. He is the author of five poetry collections, and four chapbooks of poems. He lives in Caldwell, New Jersey.

About the Lexi Rudnitsky Editor's Choice Award

The Lexi Rudnitsky Editor's Choice Award is given annually to a poetry collection by a writer who has published at least once previous book of poems. Along with the Lexi Rudnitsky First Book Prize in Poetry, it is a collaboration of Persea Books and the Lexi Rudnitsky Poetry Project. Entry guidelines for both awards are available on Persea's website (www.perseabooks.com).

Lexi Rudnitsky (1972–2005) grew up outside of Boston, and studied at Brown University and Columbia University. Her own poems exhibit both a playful love of language and a fierce conscience. Her writing appeared in *The Antioch Review, Columbia: A Journal of Literature and Art, The Nation, The New Yorker, The Paris Review, Pequod,* and *The Western Humanities Review.* In 2004, she won the Milton Kessler Memorial Prize for Poetry from *Harpur Palate.*

Lexi died suddenly in 2005, just months after the birth of her first child and the acceptance for publication of her first book of poems, *A Doorless Knocking into Night* (Mid-List Press, 2006). The Lexi Rudnitsky book prizes were created to memorialize her by promoting the type of poet and poetry in which she so spiritedly believed.

Previous winners of the Lexi Rudnitsky Editor's Choice Award:

2019   Enid Shomer, *Shoreless*
2018   Cameron Awkward-Rich, *Dispatch*
2017   Gary Young, *That's What I Thought*
2016   Heather Derr-Smith, *Thrust*
2015   Shane McCrae *The Animal Too Big to Kill*
2014   Caki Wilkinson, *The Wynona Stone Poems*
2013   Michael White, *Vermeer in Hell*
2012   Mitchell L. H. Douglas, *blak al-febet*
2011   Amy Newman, *Dear Editor*